"The game will test you, never fold. Stay ten toes down. It's not on you, it's in you and what's in you they can never take away."

– *Nipsey Hussle*

BRING OUT THE BOSS IN YOU

A 10-STEP GUIDE TO STARTING AN ONLINE BUSINESS

by

PARIS C. JACKSON

Mama, the reason I feel like I can accomplish anything I want is because of your assurance; you inspire me to better. I love you, deep.

To my big brother and first friend, thank you for being my first living example of success in our immediate family. I admire you and dream to keep making you proud. I am honored to be your keeper in life, forever.

My guardian angels, I am forever indebted.

Thank you.

Copyright © 2021 Paris C. Jackson

All rights reserved.

Contents

Preface
Introduction
Chapter One: Define Your Business
Chapter Two: Create a Name, Then Secure It
Chapter Three: Get a Logo
Chapter Four: Establish an Address
Chapter Five: Prepare to Setup Shop
Chapter Six: Content
Chapter Seven: Website
Chapter Eight: SEO
Chapter Nine: Build a Database
Chapter Ten: Marketing
Bonus: Mentorship
Epilogue

Preface

The coronavirus pandemic in 2020 really put a lot of things into perspective for me. I saw many of my friends and colleagues get laid off from their jobs, millions of people relied on government assistance to make ends meet, countless people lost their lives due to sickness, and some even took their own lives due to mental health. Living in a "shut down" city required countless people (including me) to work from home and maintain social distance. What it really did was enable us to sit with ourselves in a way that we had not before. As a result, I gained clarity on things I liked and disliked about my life at the time and what I could do to change.

Due to the pandemic, many people were no longer able to provide for themselves or not in the same capacity as before. Particularly, I noticed minorities had quickly realized financial freedom and ownership were two things that can create a more secure lifestyle and future. I began to see people tap into other parts of themselves and lean into entrepreneurship at a very beginner level. A lot of people needed supplemental income. As a former full-time entrepreneur, some of my relatives and friends depended on me and utilized my skill set as a resource for their endeavors.

I wanted to do more with my gifts to help create the life I always saw for myself while at the same time also helping others do the same. By helping my family and friends launch new businesses, I was inspired to create this 10-step guide to starting an online business so others could learn maximize their potential and be the boss of an online business too.

Before anyone goes into business, I think it's really important to know it is not an easy or quick task. At all. Starting a business is an investment of many forms. There will be long nights, countless hours of work, challenges, sacrifices and difficult times ahead. There's really no way for me to explain how the process is since everyone's journey is different. However, if you keep your mind focused on the bigger picture, have tunnel vision, don't allow negativity to get you off course, plan for all possibilities, stay prepared, continue to learn, then you will be fine!

For me, being a boss is more about mentality than anything else. Your mindset is what controls you; if you can master the power of controlling your thoughts, you will not lose. I wholeheartedly believe I can accomplish anything I set my mind to. The road may not be easy, and the path may change along the way, but the end goal is always the same. You must stay focused and remember it's a marathon, not a sprint.

I remember starting my first online business in 2012, an online hair extension company. At the same time, I was also the head manager for a multi-million-dollar retail store. I was grateful to have job security yet being micromanaged on a corporate level was one thing I strongly disliked. So, I started my business. It started small; I didn't have a clear strategy of what to do. Yes, I had a good business plan that I learned how to make in college, but I still had to use my own knowledge to figure out what to put into my plan. At the time, I didn't have any mentors with online businesses to turn to. While I lacked guidance, I was business savvy in a sense that I understood numbers and how to make money. Understanding that, in addition to my experience managing a store operation, I was able to figure out how to run my own business. I quit my salary job and brought out the boss in myself. My philosophy was "if I'm going to be overworked and underpaid, then I might as well invest in my goals instead of working for someone else's." Through years of trial and error, yet still learning as I went, I turned my small business into a 6-figure company.

Often times people who have smart, cool, profitable ideas just need a little direction, an extra push or resources. I know what that's like and that's why wrote this book; to encourage you, motivate you, guide you, and ensure you that you can be a boss too! My intention with this book is to guide as many people as I can to accomplish goals, unlock a level of financial freedom, take control of one's life. It's my way of reaching back and trying to bring as many people with me to a new way of life.

Remember, it starts in your mind, you must believe it first, then you will achieve it. Bring Out The Boss In You.

Introduction

Congratulations, and thank you for making a conscious decision to support entrepreneurship! You have made the first step of becoming a successful business owner by investing in yourself through knowledge. That alone says a lot about you. This book is enclosed with invaluable knowledge and information to help you self-start an online business and reassure current business owners. Upon completing the book, you should fully understand all 10 steps that guide you through the process of starting an online business.

When thinking of business, money is one of the first things that come to mind, yet money isn't the only fundamental tool in starting a business. Knowledge and guidance are equally as important in business as finances are. Money should be used as a tool; make your money work for you to increase your earnings exponentially. Imagine having a large sum of money and not knowing what to do with it, how to use it, or make it work for you. You would end up spending it all, and once it is gone, it is gone. There is no shortage of information; we simply must find it, which is what I mean about guidance. You must guide yourself to the knowledge and resources. The key to being successful is knowledge and guidance, along with other things, of course. Look at you, already headed in the right direction.

If you are reading this, it is because of one of two things: you have an idea for a business you want to start, but you do not know where to start, or you already have a business and want reassurance that what you have is a solid foundation for longevity.

Let us begin with the person who has an idea of a business to start. What are you going to provide? Is it a service or a product? If you want to sell clothes, juices, consulting services, catering services, it does not matter. This book will help you or reassure you through 10 fundamental steps!

If your business is already operating, use this book as a tool to sharpen your iron. Real power players understand there is always room to grow; the more you know, the more you realize how much you do not know. There is always room to learn more. As I mentioned earlier, knowledge is the key; if you continue to invest in yourself by increasing your knowledge, you will not ever fail.

So, let us get started!

Chapter One: Define Your Business

You have your idea, and you are ready to get started, but you do not really know where to begin. **Establish exactly what it is that you want to do and why.** I need you to dig deep here because this is literally the anchor for your whole business. Whether it is a hobby, a serious passion of yours, purposeful work, or literally just something you think will generate income, be intentional with it! It does not necessarily have to be your bread and butter. However, this is going to be your business, so be intentional with your mission.

Know precisely what product(s) and/or service(s) you will provide. If there are variations of what you want to do, be very specific for each. For example, when I first became an entrepreneur, I knew I wanted to sell hair extensions. That alone is a very broad goal. I had to be specific and ask myself questions. What type of hair extensions will I sell? Will I sell loose hair or wefted bundles? Should I sell wigs, frontals, and closures too? What lengths and colors? All those questions, plus many more, are what I had to ask myself to create a plan for my business. Otherwise, I would have been figuring it out more as I went, which would have taken more time and resources.

Once you have found your niche, and your offerings (aka your business), it is time to establish your goal(s) and create a business plan. Write it down and make it plain. Writing things down is a proven method to help remember things and store them in your subconscious mind. Revisit and read your goals often to keep manifesting them into fruition. Remember, being a boss starts in your mind.

Your goals' intent becomes your reason and will become your fuel on the rough days when you need motivation. We all have rough days in our personal lives, and unfortunately, it is inevitable in business. You should create both short-term and long-term goals. You want to have goals that are S.M.A.R.T.

Here is a breakdown of how to create a S.M.A.R.T. goal:

Specific: What exactly will you accomplish?

Measurable: How will you know when you have reached this goal?

Achievable: Is achieving this goal realistic with effort and commitment? Have you got the resources to achieve this goal? If not, how will you get them?

Relevant: Why is this goal significant to your life?

Timely: When will you achieve this goal?

While this is step one of the process and you may be eager to get started, stay here until you are absolutely sure what you are going to do in business. It's important to be brutally honest with yourself at the very beginning. Once you're sure, turn the page.

Chapter Two: Create a Name, Then Secure It

Now that your business is defined and you know its purpose, next you need to create a name for your brand and business, then secure it. Don't take it lightly when I say secure it. Think of your brand as your "bag" aka your money. Bosses secure the bag, so do make sure you do!

Your brand name will be what everyone will know your company as. Your business name will be how the government will know your company as a business entity (LLC, Corporation, Partnership, etc.). Sometimes these two names are the same, but as your business expands, you may tap into other endeavors and want to have separate names.

Think of many different names. Conceptualize it. Brainstorm some more. Sleep on it. The name of your business is just as powerful as every other aspect of it. It can propel you or hold you back, so think long and hard about this.

When starting a new business, it may start small, but do yourself a favor and refrain from having a small mind. Think big! Just when you think it's big, go bigger! Close your eyes and dream about it. Success is already on the way. You must believe it's possible. Think of yourself as a multi-million-dollar company!

You want your business to be unique and easily accessible. Technology has made things super accessible, which ultimately does not require as much thought and extensive research. Technology has honestly resulted in laziness to some extent. With that being said, you do not want people to have to do the most to find your business. Make your business as convenient as possible to find. Do you know anyone who likes going through hoops just to give their money to someone else? I doubt it. Make your business as convenient as possible to find.

Ask yourself the following questions and if the answer is no to any of the questions, go back to the drawing board:
- If I decide to expand, Is my brand name versatile?
- Is it professional? If I put it on a billboard, will I become embarrassed?
- Does it properly represent my business?
- Do I feel proud about this?
- Is this name available? Check availability for your business name EVERYWHERE! Check all places you want your business to live (Google, Bing, social media, etc.) to see if there is already a business in place that exists with the name you want.

As soon as someone types in the first couple letters of your brand name in a search engine (Google, Bing, etc.), you want your brand to appear. Investing in search engine optimization (SEO) will also help with this later, but for now, the focus should be on making sure your brand organically appears, and the name is unique. Learn more about SEO in Chapter Eight.

Many businesses lose potential customers due to having similar names as other businesses or special characters like underscores in their names. For example, if you are a female branding expert and want to brand yourself as a "branding queen," a few examples to stay away from are "branding.queen", "brandingqueen_," "_branding_queen." Generalized names are already widespread and including characters or symbols can create difficulty for people to land on your business by mistaking it for someone else's.

Once you have made a firm decision on a brand name, **secure it.** Remember when you checked availability? You will want to secure your name in every place that you checked. Imagine creating a million-dollar company, but not owning the name. Don't let this be you. Ownership is one of the main benefits of entrepreneurship which can grant financial freedom. Purchase a domain so that you own the website link that will direct people to your online business. The domain also has added benefits that we will discuss later in upcoming chapters.

Research different business entities (LLC, Corporation, Partnership, S-Corp, etc.), identify which one best suits your company, and then register your name as a business entity with the government.

Apply for an Employee Identification Number (EIN) if you plan to file taxes for your business. An EIN is like the business version of a Social Security Number.

It is helpful to consult a business lawyer and/or during this stage of creating a new business.

Chapter Three: Get a Logo

You have your business paperwork in order and your name secured, so now it's time to think of how people will recognize your brand. What will represent your company when there is no place for text? **You need a logo.**

A business logo is one of the core ways of making your business stand out amongst other businesses that offer similar services. A logo makes your business easily recognizable to your customers. This is majorly because people process images faster than words. Getting a logo for your business is a great way to make your business memorable. Think of the golden arch, the swoosh and the three stripes – if you saw those three images you would likely know the names of the companies they represent.

Logos help you create a recognizable brand because it is the first thing people tend to notice. The phrase "a picture is worth a thousand words" holds true when it comes to building a recognizable business. When your logo is strong and memorable, it will stay in the minds of people. This will lead to business success and longevity because the more your business stays in people's minds, the more they purchase from you and promote your products and services to others. Having a strong and memorable logo will help your new online business stand out.

Your business has an identity. This identity is what you would like people to associate with your business. This could be a professionalism that fixes problems or gives happy feelings. You can use your logo to create and communicate this unique identity. For example, let us say your online business handles food delivery. You can use your logo to communicate the happy emotions that go with eating to your advantage. You can use warm colors in your logo like orange, red, and yellow that have been proven to stimulate the appetite to attract customers to use your services.

Think of a few of the popular and successful businesses worldwide, from Amazon to Apple, who have one thing in common; a professional look that inspires trust and confidence in their ability to deliver quality service. For example, while it may seem risky to order for products to get delivered to your home address from a different location as yours, Amazon exudes professionalism that makes it easier to place that order. People have come to associate having a logo with professionalism. As a new online business, you need the trust of your target customers to grow and thrive. Make sure your logo has a professional look to it.

While the quality of your products and services are excellent, you may not get the kind of support you deserve if your business does not stand out. Without a logo, it is easy for your products to be considered generic or bootleg products that should not be purchased. Having a logo allows you to brand your product properly and makes it stand out to your customers.

A strong logo will help your business establish a good online presence. Your logo takes your website from being a generic one that could belong to any business in your industry to a dedicated website belonging to your business. Beyond your website, you can use your logo in your email marketing and your social media posts to easily capture your customers' eyes.

Now that you know how logos are beneficial to your online business, it is time to get your logo. Here are some tips to keep in mind when getting a logo:

1. **Hire a graphic designer.** If you have little or no graphic design experience, you should employ a graphic

designer to work on your business logo. Before you hire a graphic designer, you should explore multiple graphic designers and their work and select the designer whose work best suits your needs. This is important because your logo is like your company's face, and it would be on all products and materials with your business. After you have settled on a graphic designer, provide them with some creative direction. The responsibility for shaping the perception of your business and how your business is represented is **yours**. The graphic designer's job is to interpret your business's perception and bring your logo to life.

2. **Design both a text logo and a graphic logo.** Asking for this upfront will save you money and time later down the line. I've seen a lot of new businesses only have a graphic logo and later hire a designer to create a text logo too. Get it all done at once. A text logo is a type of logo with your business name in a unique font or layout, while a graphic logo is a type of logo with an image that describes your business. Alternatively, you can go for a combination logo that has both. Having both is to make the name of your business memorable so that an image can be associated with your brand. Ensure that the logo you settle for is easily printable on brand products.

3. **Secure all formats of your logo file**, not just .jpg and .png files. Having all the formats of your logo file makes it possible for you to use your logo for multiple uses, such as branded products and materials. Remember: everything you do in starting your business you need to make sure you own it.

After reading the benefits mentioned above, you should understand how having a logo is important to your business. In a nutshell, a business logo takes your business from anonymous to instantly recognizable, thus contributing significantly to your marketing efforts and leading to better sales conversion. Get a logo for your online business as soon as you can and consider registering the logo with the U.S. Patent and Trademark Office.

Chapter Four: Establish an Address

While it is true that this book was created to help you set up and run an online business effectively, just like other businesses, your online business needs a physical address associated with it. This does not mean that you need a physical business location like a storefront, restaurant, warehouse or that you necessarily *have to* operate from the physical business location. What you simply need is a business address for your mail while your business remains solely online. This provides you a return address for shipments and a place to receive business mail. A return address for shipments is required from most shipping companies before shipping your packages because your customers need to know who sent their package. If the package is not successfully delivered to the customer, it will be returned to the sender's address, which should be your business address.

For all consumer-facing mail, you will want to use an address other than your personal address. Although it might be tempting and appear easy, you should not use your personal address as your business address. Using your personal address as your business address can affect your work-life balance and bring things that should be kept strictly business into your personal space. Additionally, you might end up having unexpected guests at your home when you use your house address as your business address. Therefore, your mailing address should not be the same as your home address.

Nowadays, with so many online stores, many entrepreneurs are opting for mailbox renting. Typically, they rent post office boxes (PO box) from the United States Postal Service. While PO boxes have benefits, you should be aware of some disadvantages associated with renting. One of the major disadvantages is legitimacy. People tend to see businesses that have only PO Box addresses as illegitimate businesses that should be avoided. Though your online business is legitimate and stable, having only a PO Box address might make it appear illegitimate and unstable to your potential customers. Another disadvantage is that people may view your online business as being "too small." People often prefer to do business with businesses they consider big because it gives them a feeling of safety. Some people may be less likely to support your business if they think it is too small because you have only a PO Box address.

Gladly, with improvements in technology, there is an alternative option which could be better for you. An alternative option is having a virtual business address. A virtual business address is an address where people can find and interact with your business. A virtual business address ties a commercial address to your business.

Below are some of the benefits of having a business address:

- Professionalism: As established earlier in this guide, when people get a sense of professionalism from encountering your business, they are more likely to do business with you. As such, anything that will add to the professional look and feel of your business is great. A business address makes your business look more professional because it provides a commercial address for your business. With a virtual business address, your business address will show up as an actual address on the map instead of a rented PO Box at the post office. This will lead to greater credibility for your business.

- Effective marketing: Search Engine Optimization is a digital marketing tool that makes it easier for people to find your business online when they type keywords in your industry into their search engines such as Google. It has been shown that businesses with addresses that can be considered commercial rank higher on search engines and get greater visibility. Hence, having a business address is great for promoting your business as it communicates to people that you are easily reachable.

- Local presence: When your business has what appears to be a business address within a vicinity, it gives it some sort of local presence. So, while your business is strictly online, you have a local presence within a particular place. People tend to buy from companies that have a local presence because it communicates trustworthiness and credibility. It gives them the feeling that you are a part of them, care about them, and accessible to them. A virtual business address makes it seem like your business is domiciled in a particular location, hence creating that local presence.

- Access to traditional business services: While it may not seem like it, as your online business grows, you may eventually need some traditional business services like receptionists to take certain calls and meeting spaces for meetings with investors or even major clients. The great thing about a virtual business address is that it offers you these services. It offers you a virtual receptionist that can take calls for your business and respond to certain inquiries. It also provides you with a physical space to hold meetings at the address where your company is listed.

Now that you know the importance and benefits of having a virtual business address, here are some tips to help you set up one:

1. Select a good virtual business address solution. With more entrepreneurs and online start-ups opting for virtual business addresses, many companies offer virtual office solutions. Shop around and select one that offers you the services you want within your budget.
2. Choose a location close to you. You should pick a location close to you as your virtual business address. This offers you the ease of accessibility. Pick a place where you can easily pick up your mails or have your mails shipped to you.
3. Select the services your business needs. Do you need a virtual receptionist to take calls or orders? Do you need a physical space for occasional meetings with investors and clients? Or do you just need a professional-looking address for mailing? Whatever your needs are, be sure to select them.
4. Get a US Postal Form 1583. After you have picked the right virtual office solution for you, selected the services you need, and paid for your virtual business address, you need to get your US Postal Form 1583. Virtual business addresses require this as it authorizes commercial mail receiving companies to receive mails on your behalf.

Having a business address is a great move to make as you start your online business journey. It can make your path smoother as the credibility it gives your business attracts more patronage to your business.

Chapter Five: Prepare to Setup Shop

Organization is the part of a business that people often skip over that can save you lots of time and money along the way. This is the part where you start setting up shop before the online store is created. Your business foundation is laid, now it is time to start preparing for the concentrated work. When you have your business in order from the beginning, you will not have to backtrack later down the line. I am trying to help you make far less mistakes than I made.

Organization in business gives you a sense of purpose and direction. It is easy to feel like you are floundering in the wind when there is no organization.

"It is always the start that requires the greatest effort." – James Cash Penney, founder of J.C. Penney

Planning and organization improve the efficiency of your business as they provide an anchoring guide that helps you achieve your set goals every day. Both provide a guide that enables you to run your business's day-to-day activities and make business operations easier to carry out, thus increasing your business's efficiency.

Planning and organization will also contribute to the longevity and durability of your business. This is because they help you establish the basic framework for running your business. This framework can then be built upon to achieve the best results as you launch your business. It can also be modified as you expand operations to ensure that your business not only thrives but also stands the test of time.

Before you start operating in your business, make sure you are well equipped and prepared for basic operational functions. Create different email addresses for different business functions (i.e., customer service, each member of the team). Having a business phone can also be helpful for communicating with your customers.

If you have a home office, stock it with essential supplies such as sticky notes, pens, calendars, calculators, shipping necessities (if applicable), printer, and scanner.

Think about your branded materials and product packaging if you sell tangible products. Will you need labels to go on your products? Do you need shopping bags? What will you use to protect the products during shipping? Those are some of the questions you need to ask yourself to be prepared and organized for your online store.

Keep your business money separate from your personal money. Open a business bank account. When customers make purchases through your online business, you will need to have a bank account for your sales payments to be transferred to you to access. By keeping your business and personal finances separate, it is easier to identify how much money your business brings in. Most banks require a valid business entity and an EIN in order to open a business account. One of the main benefits of this separation is for tax purposes too. If your money is intermingled and you get audited, you might have some issues; also, if you ever get sued, your personal assets could be at stake. Of course, audits and lawsuits are two things we never want to happen, but in the beginning stages of business it is important to be prepared for any potential situations. Remember you want always to have the mindset that your business will not remain a small business, it will grow; and with new levels of success there are new challenges! Consult an accountant, tax professional and/or a business lawyer for more information; they can also give you more insight on business funding.

While you will want to have hard copies of your important documents, it is also imperative to keep a digital file of all your paperwork. We all know how abruptly things can change for a long time, so be prepared to access your business core from anywhere at any time. Having physical copies of important paperwork is always good, but what will you do if everything burns to the ground? How will your business information be protected? Imagine not being able to access your home office or workstation. One thing you can do is scan and email documents to yourself. Keep a copy of everything important in a digital place for reference. Another suggestion is to have an external hard drive – it's portable and can plug into most computers or devices. After all, who would have thought our offices and businesses would still be physically closed.

One of my favorite (and free) organizational resources is Google Drive. It is very similar to Microsoft Office for Google Account users. Utilizing spreadsheets and documents was very helpful for me. The spreadsheets are particularly beneficial (especially in the first year of business) in my professional opinion because I was able to create accounting templates to understand how my business was doing financially. Who would not want to observe if the business is profiting or losing?

Business organization should not be an uphill task. With the right tips, you will be able to expertly handle the organization of your business before you start operations and even while running the business. A few other helpful tips to stay organized and prepare for your online shop are:
- Set weekly goals based on your overall business objectives.
- Make a daily to-do list a day prior.
- Take notes any time something comes to mind and save them somewhere easily accessible. Use your notepad or

make voice memos on your cell phone to capture your thoughts to be stored in a place you can conveniently access.
- Utilize your mobile phone calendar to manage your time. Schedule all calls, meetings, and events in your calendar for planning and schedule in your to-do list for the reminders.
- Create different email address extensions for specific functions of your business (customer service, press, and staff)

Some of the best businesses are those that are proactive instead of reactive. To be proactive as a business means anticipating happenings and business trends and making decisions based on these projections. Whereas being reactive is waiting for things to happen before getting to work. Through planning and organization, you can anticipate future unfavorable situations and take necessary precautions to prevent them. Planning and organization will help you keep up with the ever-changing business trends in your industry.

Now let's dive in.

Chapter Six: Content

Digital content is a powerful tool when used correctly. Content is substantive information or creative material (in various mediums) that you will undoubtedly find necessary. The content you create (or have created) should be intended to entertain or inform while attracting potential customers. A few examples of content are visuals in the form of written texts, videos, audio-visuals, pictures, and recordings.

In today's climate, content is significant for online businesses and should not be overlooked when thinking about starting a business. Content helps build the business reputation and increase business visibility.

Engaging in digital content is a great way for you to communicate with your audience online. When you create quality content, your audience will be motivated to check out your products and become paying customers who continue to engage your content. This will provide greater publicity for your business and products. It will also be great for your brand reputation as customers will express their satisfaction with your offerings through their interaction with your content, which will result in a positive public image for your business.

In my experience, the main benefit of content creation is creating brand awareness. With today's competitive business climate, brand awareness is important because it helps your business stand out and be recognized against your competition within the same industry. When you create digital content that captures your audience's attention and causes them to interact with your brand, more people will be discussing your business and the products you offer. The more people who discuss and engage your business, the more other people will see and hear about your business. This is the goal of utilizing content.

Digital content can be used as a marketing tool through (1) quality copywriting and (2) audio-visuals.

Quality Copywriting

Some may argue that their content, such as graphics or audio-visuals, is intensive. Well, no matter the number of graphics, images, or videos in the content, **good quality copywriting** is important for effective marketing. This is because good copywriting convinces your target audience that the product you are offering can solve their needs. For example, let us say you run an insurance company. You are trying to get people to buy car insurance, putting up a billboard or a social media flier with the damaged car's image would not do the job of baiting them into your business. That flier would only be stating the problem, which will only intensify the fears of your customers. However, if you accompany the image with a text that says something like "say goodbye to worrying about your car, or X Insurance company has got your back," your target audience would be more interested in patronizing you because you have made clear what you have to offer.

Something to remember while copywriting is to ensure that your writing is tailored and suited to your target audience – as with everything you do in communicating to the public relating to your business. A tip is to use your audience's preferred language and phrases so that it resonates, and they feel connected.

Audio-visual Content

A very common way to use content is by creating audio-visuals. Audio-visuals refer to videos with sound. This could be an animated image that plays like a video and has music or voice recordings attached to it. It could be an infographic that gives your customers in-depth information about your product and includes a call to action, inviting them to reach out for further inquiries or make a buy. It could also be a video of a brand influencer unboxing your product and reviewing it.

To effectively use audio-visuals, be particular about the quality of the content. Get high-resolution videos and images and use clear soundbites or audio clips. High-quality content communicates professionalism and competence to your target customers. Your target audience should not strain their ears to get your message. Remember, you want to make things as convenient as possible for your audience. Keep the audio-visual content short and entertaining – this will capture the attention of your audience, retain it, and guide them towards making a purchase.

As a best practice, do not limit yourself to using only one method. For example, do not get stuck on just posting images. Your audience would eventually get bored. Instead, make use of all the ways to use digital content as an effective marketing tool.

Chapter Seven: Website

What's an online business without a website? Finally, it's time for yours! Setup a website – it will help establish value and boost the credibility of your business. Since your business will be online instead of a physical location, think of your website as your virtual storefront. The same website you purchased your domain from is likely to have a website builder to help you create your own website too.

In many cases, your website will be people's **first or second impression of your brand**, so make it count! Businesses that do not have websites are missing opportunities. However, a business with a bad website can give the impression that they do bad business, which is even worse than not having a website at all.

When it comes down to creating a website, you can either design it yourself or hire a professional to do it. If you decide to hire someone, be intentional with the direction you give them. Ensure your vision and ideas are properly communicated so that the website is a true reflection of your brand. Your website is the face of your brand. You will also want to make sure it is as user-friendly as possible. You know how many times I have wanted to shop with someone, but their website isn't appealing or takes too much brainpower to navigate? A lot! The more difficult it is for people to navigate your website, the less likely they will make a purchase.

Not only should your website be user-friendly for your visitors, but it should also be friendly and easy for you to navigate on the back end. Most online business owners rely on their websites to keep track of customer orders, inventory, sales reports, data, and insights. If you cannot understand your website's interfaces and functions, this will eventually reflect the quality of experience you can give your customers. Before selecting a website builder, consider all the capabilities it comes with.

Here are a few things your website should include both **for your visitors' benefit** and **for your benefit**:

For your visitors (as applicable)
- Branded content, mission, tagline/slogan
- Menu Navigation
- Scheduling capabilities if you offer services
- Product images
- Product descriptions
- Price
- Customer reviews and testimonials
- Frequently asked questions
- Shipping & Returns Policy
- Contact information
- Links to social media

For your business
- Data collection
- Photo & Video functionality
- Inventory tracking & threshold notifications
- Sales analytics reports
- 3rd party merchant so that you can accept payments on your website

As you continue through this 10-step guide, you will learn so much about how to attract people to your website and how to turn visitors into paying customers. Your website and digital marketing strategy will give you the ability to market your business online. It is very integral to position yourself online with a strong, beautifully presented, and easy to navigate digital store that effectively represents your products and services. Make sure your website motivates people to want to shop with you. You will learn how to analyze your website traffic by demographics to understand the type of people your business attracts.

Chapter Eight: SEO

Once you have a live published website, you will need to drive traffic to the site to increase visibility and awareness. Each person that visits your site is a potential customer. The more visitors to your online shop, means more chances of making sales – this is also known as conversion. You may be wondering how you can get more people to your website, and the answer is search engine optimization.

Search Engine Optimization or SEO is used to optimize a website to attract more website visitors from the free organic results on search engines such as Google, Bing, and others. These search engines also play a significant role in the shopping decision of digital consumers. For instance, when potential customers search products online using Google, and they do not find you there, chances are, they will never learn about your business.

SEO allows businesses to connect with the target market at the right place and time, playing a significant role in the consumers' shopping decisions online. Therefore, SEO aims to get your business website to rank at the top of Search Engine Result Pages (SERP) by following search engine guidelines and ultimately improving your website's quality. Search engines make these rules or guidelines to determine whether a website's content is worth showing on its SERP.

When people search a keyword on the internet, there are numerous results for countless search queries. To rank them, search engines use algorithmic factors, including quality of posts, page structures, number of inbound and outbound links, and more. As such, an optimized website that makes use of these algorithmic factors will rank above non-optimized websites on the SERP.

If you still do not understand why SEO is so important, here are some of the top benefits below:

1. Higher Rankings and Increased Organic Traffic: As mentioned above, one of the most rewarding benefits of SEO is improving the rankings of a website on the SERP. And when a website page is within the first five organic search results on the first page of the SERP, it gains a click-through rate of 67.60%, thus increasing its organic traffic. Also, 30% of this click-through rate falls to the top 1 position. This is due to the consumers who expect that the top search results offer high-quality information.

2. Better User Experience: A website that provides its visitors with the best customer experience likely has a higher ranking. If your website visitors are looking for answers for a certain topic or looking to buy your products, you should aim to provide a seamless experience. Websites with mediocre user experience or are slow loading tend to have a higher bounce rate (number of users who click on the website, then leaving without further transactions). It is a metric that signals search engines that a website is low-quality, thus demoting its ranking – you do not want that.

3. Reach the target market at the right place and time: Search engines provide personalized search results to their users based on their past search history, location, and other online activities. It is indeed a useful tool for businesses to drive quality traffic to their websites. This is especially true for local businesses who aim to reach locals to buy their products and services.

Chapter Nine: Build a Database

As you start your online business, you will begin to attract customers and drive traffic to your site. Once you drive traffic to your site, you should save their information. This is a gem, truly. It will come in handy both in the short term and in the long term.

A database is the storage of people's contact information; this can include first and last name, email, phone number, location, and more (or less). Databases have other names like mailing lists or newsletters. A database can be like intangible GOLD. Once you fully grasp this, you will start to notice that many online websites offer incentives to encourage people to sign up for newsletters or mailing lists.

Databases are helpful when you want to reach your audience quickly and stay engaged. One of the main benefits of having a database is having a quick, convenient way to reach an audience. As a new business, you can import your contacts from your phone and email to create a database and send an email or text to announce the launch of your new business. This way, your target customers can see your new business and support you. You can also use the database for when you are having a sale. Some members of your target audience may not see your social media posts announcing your sale. However, when you send a direct text or email about your sale to your target audience, they are more likely to respond and participate in the sale.

Databases also help you build better customer relationships. This is because databases help you gather information on your target customers, which will help you understand them. With the right information on your customers, you will understand their purchasing habits, needs, and type of service they desire. Understanding your customers will help you better target them. A database will give you insight into who your top customers are. Based on your understanding of who they are, you can create special offers, discounts, or rewards schemes for them. This can be a great business marketing tactic because as more people find out about your rewards schemes or discounts for your top customers, they will bring more business your way so they can have access to these benefits.

A database can very much become your leverage as your business expands. As your business grows, you may consider forming a partnership or a collaborative effort with another company or a group of companies. Your database contains customer information, which is necessary for business targeting and driving sales. This information will be beneficial to the company you are trying to form a partnership with, and it can get you the most favorable partnership terms.

From time to time, it is good to take a step back and analyze the progress of your online business. Typically, this is referred to as "taking stock." Here, you look at your products and identify what products are selling better, what marketing strategy is working for your business, and what type of customers support your business the most. This is a necessity. While you can do this manually, this can be time-consuming. Having a database gives you a single location to access this information and find valuable information that will help you develop better products and improve your customer service.

"*Data beats emotions.*" – Sean Rad, founder of Tinder

Seeing how beneficial having a database is, below are a few tips that can help you set up a database for your online business:

- The simplest way to create an organic database as a new online business is to capture your customers' data every time they make a purchase from you. Since your business is online, getting this data is easier. As customers click on your online link or visit your online store to make a purchase, put in place a pop-up form they must fill to complete the purchase. This form should contain spaces for them to fill in the information you need about them. Mostly information that gives you better access to them and an understanding of your target demographic such as name, age, email, phone number, and location.
- If your business is yet to launch officially and you are yet to make sales, apart from adding people from your contact list to your mailing list, a great way to create a database as a start-up company is to encourage people to sign up for your mailing list to "be first to know" when your business launches.

Mailchimp is a great resource to start your database and engage with your audience through email marketing. You can upload your existing contacts to Mailchimp, create special mailing lists depending on the different categories of customers you have. Leverage your database as soon as possible to get greater access to your customers and increase sales conversion.

Chapter Ten: Marketing

Imagine you are shopping on a retailer's online website, and you find two different brands that sell the exact same type of product that you are looking for at the same exact price, but you can only afford to purchase one. How will you determine which product to buy? The difference between who gets the sale can simply come down to marketing. Whichever brand does it best will win the sale, and your efforts will be worth it.

What is marketing? Marketing is basically all activities a brand does to advertise and sell services or products to people. It offers a link between your business and your target market that gives an edge over your competition. When brands can connect with potential and existing customers, communicate effectively with them, and elicit brand loyalty, it is safe to say that they will occupy a larger share in the industry.

Being a leader in your industry can be made possible simply by investing in marketing. Sometimes it takes years for companies to really understand what their customers want from them – a lot of trial and error.

As a new business owner, it is important that you have a good understanding of what your customers want and hope to get when they shop with you. You should have a good understanding of the experience they are paying for and how best to make that experience available to them. This way, not only will your business become a favorite within your niche, but also, when you decide to scale and expand your business, you can implement the knowledge you have on what your customers want. Once you know what they want, you create a marketing strategy to communicate what your business offers effectively. There are four parts to a **marketing mix: product, price, place, and promotion**. This is also known as "the four P's" and should be referenced when creating your marketing strategy.

For a start-up, marketing can seem a bit intimidating. However, it is not as complicated as it looks.

With this guide, your new business will do great leveraging on the power of good marketing, and here are several reasons why:

- **Reach the right target audience** – digital marketing platforms and tools have helped businesses segment their audience and reach the right ones. By keeping track of a potential customer's online activities and demographic information, you can offer your products to specific customers who are known to be interested in those products like yours. Some tools allow businesses to keep track of a customer's buying stage. For example, if an online shopping customer added a specific product into their carts but did not proceed to check out, you can use this information to advertise that product to the customer.
- **Inform your audience** – people prefer the safety of informed purchasing. When people are well-versed on products and their uses or services and benefits, they can make a more informed decision at the purchase point. No one wants to feel like they are walking into a trap when they purchase goods or services. By keeping this in mind, you can comfortably use marketing to establish a good communication channel that helps you provide both your existing customers and your potential customers with the right information they need.
- **Promotes customer engagement** – by offering your customers information about your products and delivering custom content, they will become more receptive and likely to leave product reviews.

Reviews are one of the easiest ways to learn more about your customers' preferences. However, there will be no customers to give you the reviews you need if you do not market to them. Hence, marketing is an essential part of building a successful business because it brings your customers closer to you by creating the opportunity for them to express their wants, needs, and desires to you.

- **Boosts sales** – when you position your products and services in front of your audience, the more people who see your products translate to more sales. It is possible for you to earn a sale simply because of the **place** it is located (one of the 4 P's) where your competition may not be.
- **Better conversion rates** – you want to increase traffic to your online store and convert those viewers to paying customers. For example, if you launch an email marketing campaign, you will know how many customers clicked through the email and completed a website transaction (e.g., purchased an advertised product). It is a collection of data that you can use to make better campaigns proven to convert visitors to paying customers.
- **Strengthens your brand reputation in the industry** – continuing to market your business directly influences growth and longevity over time; it ensures sustainability through building its social standing and relevance. Additionally, marketing comes in handy with branding and PR strategies that help maintain your business's reputation.
- **Build rapport** – people want to patronize businesses that appear to genuinely care about them and their needs. For this reason, it is important that you build a proper rapport, and marketing makes this possible. Through marketing campaigns that express your willingness and desire to meet your customers' needs and offer them a means of contacting you for

further correspondence, you can effectively build a good consumer-business relationship. For example, let's say you run a home cleaning service. Your marketing campaign could include social media posts that offer your clients viable home tips and emails that introduce them to your service and how it can make their lives easier and better. With these, you have established that you care enough about their well-being and making their lives better. This will then motivate them to patronize you as opposed to patronizing another brand that feels impersonal. Building a strong rapport will give you loyal customers who will make more purchases and introduce your goods and services to their friends and loved ones.

- **Elicit brand loyalty and retention**– strategically promoting your products to your existing customers with incentives can result in repeat customers and having a quality product can result in your brand being a top choice for people in the market. Retaining existing customers (a.k.a, repeat customers) costs less than attracting and converting new ones. Although gaining customer loyalty is one of the most desired benefits of digital marketing, it is very difficult to obtain. Nonetheless, it is a valuable effort that provides many benefits to the business in the end. Digital marketing increases customer engagement either through personalized email offers or, more commonly, in social media. These are two efforts that are proven to increase customer loyalty.
- **Informed business owner decisions** – informative qualities of marketing also extend to you as the business owner. You should monitor how your marketing efforts are going. Based on how your audience responds to your marketing efforts, you

can adjust your marketing strategy and your product or service offerings.

Digital marketing especially will be important for your online business. It is simply the marketing efforts of a business done online. Digital marketing is basically an easier and more cost-effective way to reach your target audience. It is also exceptionally valuable for ensuring your business's sustainability by building its social standing and relevance.

Digital content creation opens you up to a whole world of effective and efficient marketing. It enables your marketing effort to easily capture the attention of the right people who would become loyal customers, helping you get greater patronage through personal marketing.

Before the rise in e-commerce, traditional marketing strategies included: televisions, radios, magazines, events, and even direct mail. Those methods have all proven to be effective, and however, with the increase in e-commerce, digital marketing has taken advertising to a new level on the internet.

There are numerous strategies you can use to market your business online. Some strategies include paid search, display advertising, social media, content, email, influencer, affiliate marketing, mobile applications, and search engine optimization (SEO). With more people spending their time online, entrepreneurs now have a more effective and less costly channel to reach our target market. To stay ahead of the competition in this era, SEO and social media should always be utilized. These are two strategies that allow businesses to connect with the target market at the right place and time, playing a significant role in the consumers' shopping decisions online.

Social Media

Thanks to the connectivity empowered by the internet, the world is becoming a global village. With social media's help, it seems like the world has become a smaller place due to the ease of access and closer reach. Let's be honest, the internet and social media have changed the game for businesses – especially influencer marketing. Right now, in most cases, social media is one of the best ways to reach a diverse group of people who somehow fit into your target market or demographic. Create social media accounts on all relevant platforms for your business even if you do not see a fit currently; it may be useful in the future.

Social media can really be valuable in promoting your business by increasing brand visibility, creating a buzz, and even as a method of providing customer service and increasing your brand's credibility and reputation. Make sure you create accounts for your brand on all relevant social media channels. Below are three ways you can use social media as an effective marketing tool:

1. **Get Brand Recognition**: Your business needs to be recognizable by your target market. What this means is that your customers need to be more familiar with your business to the point of actively seeking out your business because they recognize it. This is because, unlike traditional media that presents your brand to a smaller list of people, social media puts your brand in front of many more people quickly and easily. It introduces people to your brand even when they are not looking for the product you are selling.
    a. Practice strategic logo placement. Post pictures with your business' logo somewhere on the image. Begin your videos with your business' logo or place it in a visible corner of the video. With well-placed logos of your business on your social media pages (preferably Twitter and Instagram), you can keep your business in the

mind of your customers and make your brand easily recognizable.
   b. Posting product and brand unveiling videos on your social media pages can also gain recognition. Visual content is essential for creating brand awareness on social media because people are attracted to what they can see. Adding audio content to the visual content helps keep their attention. In creating videos, try to capture their attention in the first 15 seconds seeing as there may be other things vying for their attention. You should also make the video short, so you do not take up much of their time, keep them engaged during their small attention span, and so they look forward to more videos from you.
2. **Create a Buzz**: The world thrives on conversations, and as more people connect online, more conversations are being had. You should use social media to create a conversation around your business. Creating a buzz will position your business for greater patronage. You can create a buzz by asking for feedback on your products through fun online polls, talking about an issue related to the products you sell, or even giving shout outs to other businesses you work with.
3. **Provide Great Customer Service**: One of the best ways to market your business is by providing excellent customer service. People will be drawn to patronize simply because they can vouch for your customer service quality, which makes them feel safe enough in their decision to give their money to you.
   a. Offering great customer service via social media is as simple as being available to politely respond to complaints and inquiries within the shortest time possible; you can also have a dedicated social media manager to respond for

you. The direct message feature of most social media platforms can be used to achieve this.
  b. Giving personalized replies to your customers' comments on your social media posts is another good way to provide service.
4. **Ensure Conversions**: The major aim of marketing efforts is conversion, taking your target audience from the starting point of being potential customers to the endpoint of being paying customers.
  a. With social media, you can promote conversion by **adding calls to action,** which motivates your target audience to carry out an action, in this case, to patronize your business. For example, on an Instagram or Twitter post, you can ask them to send a DM to make a purchase or call a number attached to your post.
  b. You can also ensure conversion by **organizing contests and giveaways,** which gets more traffic to your business and causes people to make purchases in the process. For example, let us say you own a clothing line, and you would love to get more people to see your staple piece. You can ask people to repost a picture of the item on social media, and the person whose post has the highest number of engagement (likes, retweets, or comments) will win the item. This way, more people will share your product, more people will follow your business on social media, and more people will purchase your product.
  c. Another way for you to ensure conversion is by running **sponsored pay-per-click ads** on Facebook, Instagram, and Twitter. You can run sponsored ads that get people to click on the call to action to either land on your social media page, visit your website, or make a direct purchase.

All the above methods of using social media as a tool for marketing work hand in hand. Combine different methods to get the best marketing results. Two things to remember are: marketing thrives on digital content and factor marketing expenses into your business plan.

Bonus: Mentorship

Remember what I stated about knowledge and guidance? Apply it. Guidance is so important in business. It is almost better to start with no money and some guidance than no guidance and some money. I spent so much money just trying things out without a clear plan. To get the guidance you need for your brand, I strongly suggest seeking mentorship.

> *"There's no shortage of information; there's a shortage of guidance."* – Spectacular Smith

One of the best ways to achieve greater performance and productivity in business is to involve someone else through mentorship. A mentor can help boost your performance and productivity by offering ideas, advice, support, and guidance to set your business in the right direction. In addition, a mentor will also help you identify the areas you need to pay greater attention to, the places you need to invest greater resources in, and guide you towards making the best choices for your business.

A business mentor can help you view situations and issues from perspectives that are different from yours. These might be perspectives you never considered or perspectives you considered but chose to overlook. For example, at the start of your online business journey, you might struggle with viewing your business through the eyes of a customer or a potential investor. A business mentor, who has greater experience dealing with customers and investors, can provide much-needed insight into how customers or investors view your business and help you make important business decisions based on this.

Having access to a larger network is often beneficial to businesses. This is because a larger network means greater reach, which results in increased sales. Apart from more sales, the more people you meet through having a larger network, the greater the odds that you will meet people who can help you solve some problems that may arise as your online business takes off and grows. A business mentor can connect you with more people who can make your business thrive. For example, your business mentor can introduce someone in his network looking to invest in a start-up like yours. They can also introduce you to people who will offer you the best services in terms of things you need to set up your online business, such as web design for your new company.

Beyond serving as an adviser and a consultant for your business, a business mentor can also help you develop and hone your business skills. They can look at an area that you struggle with and help you develop the skills to better handle that area of business. For example, let us say you may be struggling to clearly communicate your brand identity as a new online business. Your business mentor can work with you to improve your brand communication skills and help you get better at expressing your brand identity in a way that your customers can easily recognize and identify with. This way, you will have better brand communication skills both now and in the future.

Now that the benefits of mentorship in business have been established, here are some tips to help you pick the right business mentor:

- Identify a mentor you can trust to lead you upward, someone who has more business knowledge and experience than you. This is important because it might be difficult to respect someone who does not have enough business experience to mentor you. If you would not trade places with them, do not trust exactly what they are saying unless it is proven to have worked. Business knowledge is often easily acquirable from reading business resources online. However, you do not want to be mentored by a person who can regurgitate business knowledge garnered from books and articles. You want to be mentored by someone who has real-life business experience. This person should have put in the time and the work to build that experience. They should have encountered failure and hindrances to some extent. They should have scaled hurdles to reach success. You should go for someone who has entrepreneurial growth and has spent a considerable amount of time in your industry and in business.

- Be mindful of your personality and the type of person you will look to as a mentor. Ensure that your values align. As a new entrepreneur, you should pick a mentor who shares similar values with you. This will make it easier for you to be more comfortable and less guarded with your mentor, essentially making it easier for your mentor to offer you the guidance and support you need. Have a brief pre-mentoring conversation with a potential mentor before deciding whether you want them to be your business mentor or not. In that brief conversation, learn more about their values and belief system, especially regarding issues that are dear to your heart.
- Pick someone you trust. It is difficult to learn from someone you do not trust. As such, you should ensure that your mentor is someone you can trust. When it comes to trusting your mentor, it does not stop at trusting them with issues and problems you would not share with anyone else. You should also be able to trust that they have your best interests at heart and that they will not offer you advice that will negatively affect your business. Trusting your mentor makes it easy for you to let them guide you and apply their advice to situations.

At the end of the day, your mentor should be someone you trust and respect.

Epilogue

This guide has thus far provided you a clear and concise landscape view of what it takes to start an online business.

Starting a business is no easy feat. However, having an actionable guide that breaks down the process into steps can make the process so much smoother versus trying to figure it out as you go. Defining your business is a huge part of its success – your business should have a purpose, and you should have a good thorough understanding of your target audience.

Key things to remember:
1. Utilize your resources and have patience.
2. Delegate duties where you can afford to.
3. Creating a unique brand name that properly represents your business means nothing if you cannot secure rights to the name and fully own it. Take your time and establish your business structure the right way that best suits you.
4. Establishing boundaries between you as a person and you as a business owner is a great practice to implement early in business.
5. Organization might be implied to most and may seem like a no-brainer, but this is the key to having a business that will stand the test of time. Strategically plan everything!
6. Creating quality content can make or break your brand image, your website, and all your marketing efforts.
7. Marketing is tough yet rewarding. It can help you build a thriving business. As such, it is important for you to put an excellent marketing strategy in place for your business. After learning what marketing can do for your business, how social media is an excellent tool, and

practical digital content creation tips, you have enough guidance to get your business online.
8. Continue learning and investing in your growth and development.
9. Never take no for an answer!

I applaud you for investing in yourself through knowledge. I wish you longevity and success in your business endeavors and am honored to have been able to contribute to your value. I look forward to seeing how you implement the resources this book offers you into your business. For additional resources, visit parischane.com.

10-STEP CHECKLIST

I defined my business ☐

I created a name and secured it ☐

I have a logo ☐

I have a business address ☐

My business foundation is prepared ☐

I have content ☐

I have a website ☐

I have SEO ☐

I created a database ☐

I can market my business ☐

Made in the USA
Monee, IL
01 May 2021